Like the Wideness of the Sea

Like the Wideness of the Sea

Maggi Dawn

Women Bishops and the Church of England

DARTON·LONGMAN+TODD

First published in 2013 by
Darton, Longman and Todd Ltd
1 Spencer Court
140 – 142 Wandsworth High Street
London SW18 4JJ

ISBN: 978-0-232-53001-8

Phototypeset by Kerrypress Ltd, Luton, Bedfordshire.
Printed and bound by Bell & Bain, Glasgow.

Contents

Introduction

... as every one knows, meditation and water are wedded for ever.

Herman Melville, *Moby Dick*

I love the water. If I need to find a new direction of thought, if I need to recover my creative thinking, then top of my agenda will be a trip to the seashore. The beach is like a liminal space between daily life and the mystery of the deep; the ebb and flow of the tide measuring time in a powerful, dignified way. Like the repeating pattern of the Daily Offices, it seems the same and yet is never exactly the same as the day before; although it is changing constantly, those changes are almost imperceptible to the human eye. The English Channel, the North Sea, the Atlantic: in all my favourite places, these bodies of water change the landscape in tiny increments. Here, then, I find a picture of God that is at once constant yet not static, dependably predictable while my own life unfolds year by year. Summer or winter, the water's edge is a cathedral in the open spaces, a place that restores perspective, where the mental cobwebs are blown away, and where I can think clearly and catch the whispers of God's voice.

I spent a good bit of time beach walking in the early 1990s, considering a renewed pull towards a sense of vocation that had tugged at my heartstrings ever since my mid-teens but which had never been possible. At last, it seemed, the Church of England might ordain women as priests. Some time later, after the General Synod of November 1992, and after a personal journey that involved much reading, talking and prayer, I sat alone on an English beach in south-west England where the Atlantic tides wash in, looking out across the sea, and agreed with myself and with God that I would accept the Church's call to become a priest.

It was nearly two decades later, in 2010, that I stood on the same beach trying to resolve a dilemma. I had grown into my vocation, for the most part fulfilled it well, and loved the people that it led me to. My dilemma, then, did not concern my sense of calling to the work I did, for that was stronger than ever. Rather, it concerned whether it was possible or even desirable to continue doing it in a church that, two decades later, still had not found a way of fully authenticating the ministry of women. It was a difficult decision, as I shall explain later, but on that beach in 2010 I came to the conclusion that, for a time at least, I should remove myself from public ministry in the Church of England. I didn't know how to begin, or where it would lead me, and it took me some months to find a way forward. But what I least expected was that by the time General Synod returned to the legislation in late 2012 I would be watching it from the other side of the same ocean, in a new situation where no such prejudice prevails. And though I had hoped that a change might restore my perspective, I really had no idea of the depth of impact it would have on me, both personally and professionally, to be treated simply as a priest, not as a 'woman priest'.

In this book, then, I shall offer three reflections. The first is a brief synopsis of the history of the process and debate concerning the ordination of women, and some thoughts on its theological aspects. The theological arguments for and against women becoming priests and bishops have been rehearsed so endlessly that it would be reasonable to ask whether there is anything more to say about them. Rather than reiterate all those irreconcilable views, I simply want to suggest a point of focus that might offer a way to break the deadlock.

In the second chapter I shall offer some thoughts on the spirituality of waiting. We are told often, and with a depth of spiritual earnestness, that the correct Christian response to a situation such as this is to return to prayer, to wait on God and to wait for God's time. Waiting is a central thread in Christian belief and practice, but misapplied it can be distorted into a rhetoric of waiting as a means of silencing protest. I want to explore the idea that we are mistakenly urging each other to wait for God while the possibility hangs in the air that God is waiting for us.

My third reflection is an account of my own unfolding vocation. I am just the right age to have grown up being told that women could never be priests, then, in early adulthood, to have seen that door opened and subsequently to see it half-closed again. As my male peers begin to fill the seats in the House of Bishops, I find myself looking at an institution which states on the one hand that it wishes to include women, yet maintains legislation that for the most part keeps them subservient to men when they should be serving alongside them.

Discussions held in Synod usually concern the practical and theological outworking of proposed legislation. But there are not many platforms for the lived experience of women who have been ordained, and it largely goes unheard that many of us have been living with daily expressions of serious and unacceptable prejudice which have produced highly-stressed working situations for many female clergy.

An enormous amount of consideration is given to the consequences, should women become fully integrated into the clergy, for male priests and for congregations who cannot accept women as priests or bishops. The possibility that they might feel compelled to leave the Church of England has been the source of many revisions and amendments to the pending decision to include women fully, and no doubt it is right that this should be so. Yet scant attention is given to those men and women who, for the lack of the inclusion of women, have already felt compelled to leave. In saying this I have no intention of making threats or demands, but I believe it is important to put on record that for me and for a number of other clergy and lay people, male and female, the current situation is not just a conundrum about making everyone happy. It is an impasse that projects such an unacceptable and illogical theological message that real people are currently withdrawing their presence from the Church. If it really matters to the Church that people do not leave over this issue, those who are already leaving, quietly and without making demands, need to be noticed just as much as the few who threaten to leave unless adequate provisions are made for them.

It is, perhaps, also important to put into print some of my experiences of two decades in the Church, to present first-hand what it has been like to negotiate my own sense of calling before, during and after the Synod decisions of the past twenty years, and why I eventually arrived at the conviction that leaving was not only compatible with my vocation, but essential to it. The ability to live out one's calling depends not only on the willingness of the Church to ordain, but on an environment that makes working within the Church possible as a daily reality. Prejudice against women is more vocal and more prevalent than many would like to believe, and if we do move towards consecrating women, then we will need more than a piece of legislation; we will need to give focused attention to changing the culture of the Church.

Having left quietly, and with the sorrow but also the blessing of my Bishops in England, I now see the situation from a different perspective. While I lived in the midst of the discussions, with their immediate personal implications, the issues seemed enormously complicated. But from the other side of the ocean, perhaps due to having some distance from the situation and no longer feeling weighed down by it, I now see the priorities with a fresh clarity. Whether this will make any difference at all to those who are making the decisions I cannot predict. But I hope, at least, that it will offer a thread of hope to those other clergy and laypersons, male and female, who, like me, have found themselves in a quandary about their own future in the Church.

These themes are in places rather sombre. To recount honestly the experience of living with unacceptable levels of prejudice may not make for a pleasant read, and I have thought much about whether I should write it down at all. But in the end this is not an angry book, or a sad one, because I am neither angry nor sad. I feel immensely fortunate, and full of hope, as I shall explain further in Chapter 3. Anyone speaking or writing about the Gospel will always end up speaking of hope, and this is, ultimately, a book about hope. It is impossible to speak of that hope without telling the truth but, looking back from the other side of the ocean, having taken a tough decision, what I have discovered is not sorrow or regret, but fresh hope that comes from discovering afresh the breadth of God's kindness and mercy. As the hymn from which this book's title is taken says, *there's a wideness in God's mercy, like the wideness of the sea*. It is this hope that I wish to offer with these thoughts.

Chapter 1

A Theological Impasse

Day after day, day after day,
We stuck, nor breath nor motion;
As idle as a painted ship
Upon a painted ocean.
        Samuel Taylor Coleridge,
        The Rime of the Ancient Mariner

The debate surrounding the ordination and consecration of women has been going on for a long time, in painfully slow steps. Sometimes slowness is a good thing. Significant decisions that affect thousands should usually not be made in a hurry. But this particular debate has lost the sense of slow but worthwhile progress. Instead it has been going round in circles, giving the appearance of moving while actually standing still. With every delay and every failure to reach resolution, we have been urged to pray more, wait longer and reconsider, as if there is some further revelation to discover, some theology we haven't yet thought of, that might be the answer to the problem. But we seem more than ever to be at an impasse, while the same arguments are rehearsed again and again. Perhaps the time has passed for attempting to add weight to one theological argument over another. Perhaps the more vital question to ask is how such deadlock was reached, and what would lead us out of it.

There is a poem in the English language, redolent with theological meaning, that explores ideas of sin and human failing, community wellbeing and individual calling, time and eternity, continuity and change at a time of rapid cultural development. Right at the heart of the poem is a story of a ship steering into a situation of deadlock, lost in a spiritual backwater and unable to move forwards or back. Although the poem was thought of as quaintly old-fashioned even when it was written, it has endured as a tale of human survival after deep conflict, and has striking parallels with the situation the Church of England has steered into over the issue of women and ordination.

The poem is Coleridge's *The Rime of the Ancient Mariner*. The Mariner narrates the tale, and tells of how the ship set sail in clear weather, but somewhere south of the equator steered into difficult waters. Moving slowly, and narrowly avoiding danger, the sailors were guided by an albatross, who proved to be both an emblem of good luck and a gentle guide through the cold and icy seas. But the Mariner confesses that, inexplicably, he committed an apparently motiveless crime: he shot the albatross. A dread superstition then enveloped the whole crew; in hostility born of fear, they hung the dead albatross around the Mariner's neck, and then, seemingly, the ship sailed over an invisible line into another dimension where all natural order was inverted. The ship sat still on the ocean; surrounded by water yet dry as a bone, under an oppressive midday sun that never moved from the sky, it was isolated and immobilised while the heat bore down upon it. For Coleridge, the sun did not represent a holy clarity, but a fearsome intensity, and, under this oppressive sun, supernatural characters began to intervene in the narrative until the Mariner found himself bargaining with strange spectres while one by one his crew fell dead around him on the decks. There seemed no way forwards or back. When the Mariner saw sea snakes swimming alongside the ship, initially they horrified him and he thought they represented yet another layer of punishment. But then he recognised their inherent beauty, because they were living things, and at once the spell was broken, the ship moved back into the dimension of the natural world and he was able to complete the voyage, returning home a changed and a chastened man, but wiser and happier.

Much of the imagery in the Ancient Mariner is ambiguous and suggests multiple interpretations. But what is clear is the shape of the narrative. The voyage out leads to the point at which everything goes wrong; the return journey sees the Mariner reaching the shores of his homeland; and, in between, the ship is mysteriously transported into the supernatural dimension, where it is paralysed. Here the Mariner is frozen in time as every strand of hope to which he clings fails him, and nothing he attempts can move him back to his true voyage. No explanation is ever offered as to his motive for shooting the albatross, whether accident, malice aforethought, murderous intent or spur-of-the-moment destructive impulse; neither is it ever quite clear whether his arrested time in the strange ocean is punishment, or mere loss of direction. The point of the poem, though, is not to explain the cause of the misadventure, but to relate the experience of paralysis and transformation.

Here, then, is a poetic rendering of a situation in which, without a clear voice on what the problem is or where the fault lies, an institution arrives at a point of paralysis, which it seems powerless to resolve. Like the Mariner's ship, the Church of England seems to have crossed a line; instead of moving anywhere we are thrashing about in a fog of frustration, fear, guilt and subdued anger, trying to pretend we are moving forward, but in reality standing still, with casualties beginning to mount up, and with a stench of decay beginning to hang over the whole affair. As in the poem, apportioning blame is as impossible as it is pointless; the real question is how to find the vision that will free us from the mess. And when the answer comes, it is likely to be surprisingly simple, but full of life.

Nothing new under the sun

There are some who dispute the idea that we are at an 'impasse' as such, and have argued that the idea of ordained women is still so new that any delay represents nothing more than a pinprick of time in the lengthy history of the Church. But this is a failure to recognise that the discussion of the ministry of women dates back at least as far as the New Testament, and has many significant moments throughout medieval and modern history, the substance of which would fill many books. The debate itself is not new, and neither are the current arguments for the acceptance of women merely a novelty of feminist theology, as some suggest. The reasoning that currently goes back and forth about priesthood, sacrament and the suitability of women to the task of leadership or sacramental representation have been rehearsed before now in different contexts, but with the essence of the argument being strikingly similar – William Tyndale's debates with Thomas More in the 1520s and 1530s being striking examples. Starting with the assertion that it was the elements of communion that were sacrament, not the priesthood itself, and emphasising the idea that women as well as men were included in the 'priesthood of all believers', Tyndale stated that women could, where necessary, celebrate the Eucharist.[1] He drew on Christ's injunction to 'love thy neighbour as thyself' to suggest that women would not be judged for celebrating the sacraments; furthermore, he wrote, women were permitted to baptise in cases of emergency, so if they could administer one sacrament, why not the other also?

(It is perhaps worth noting too that the tendency for such debates to lose their focus is also nothing new. Dialogue between Tyndale and More was lengthy, and More's *Confutation of Tyndale's Answer* is colourfully described by one author as 'an interminable desert, stretching to a hellish horizon under the untempered sun, and we find burning on every page a monotonous fury that deadens the soul.'[2])

Tyndale was not arguing for the ordination of women, but analysing the relationship between church, sacrament and human representation; furthermore, the logical conclusion of his argument could be that anyone, ordained or not, could celebrate and administer the sacraments in the absence of a priest. Nevertheless, his *Answer to Sir Thomas More's Dialogue* elegantly demonstrates that the past twenty years of theological arguments concerning women's involvement in the sacraments are by no means novel within theological debate, and cannot be dismissed as postmodern, feminist or the result of secularism.

A brief history

The most recent chapter of the debate is not a novelty dating back a mere two decades, nor is the current deadlock a momentary inconvenience. It can only be properly understood in the light of the history of formalised ministry for women in the Church of England, which began over a hundred and fifty years ago with the beginning of the Deaconess Movement[3].

Elizabeth Ferard[4] was the first woman to be licensed as a deaconess in the Church of England, in July 1862. With the encouragement of Archibald Tait, then Bishop of London, she had visited the fledgling Deaconess Movement in Germany, and on her return gathered together a group of like-minded women who together committed themselves to the service of the Church in the Community of St Andrew – a residential community of deaconesses founded to minister to the poor of London's parishes. Isabella Gilmore[5] became a deaconess in 1887, and under her leadership the movement expanded beyond residential communities to become parish-based, and deaconesses became 'a curiously effective combination of nurse, social worker and amateur policemen'.[6]

As the Deaconess Movement spread throughout the country and worldwide, interest was kindled in the idea of the ordination of women. In the years leading up to the First World War, Maude Royden[7] became active in the campaign for women's suffrage, and was also outspoken in urging the Church to open ministry up to women. 'The Church [of England] should go forward along the path of progress,' Royden said in a speech in 1917, 'and be no longer satisfied only to represent the Conservative Party at prayer.'[8] The same year, as the pulpits of the Church of England remained firmly closed to women, Royden accepted a post as Assistant Preacher at the City Temple, a non-conformist church in London. In England, campaigns for women's equality in both national and Church life were mostly abandoned during the war years, but in 1929, just one year after women received the vote on an equal footing with men,[9] Royden founded the Society for the Ministry of Women. This, following as it did from the development of the Deaconess Movement, is often thought of as the official start of the campaign for the ordination of women. Royden herself was the first woman to become a Doctor of Divinity in 1931, and continued to preach all over the world in the years between the wars.

The Church of England continued to license deaconesses, but the ordination of women was not given further serious consideration by the Church of England until a Church Assembly report of 1966. Consultation with the dioceses then took place, and in 1975 the General Synod resolved that 'there are no fundamental objections to the ordination of women to the priesthood'. Despite that, no movement was made to proceed with legislation at that time, as the general mood was considered ambivalent. In response to this, the Movement for the Ordination of Women was formed, and continued to campaign until women were eventually ordained to the priesthood.

After the 1975 Synod, more than a decade passed before women were ordained as permanent deacons in 1987, and, after another hiatus, Synod agreed in 1992 that women would be ordained as priests. Resolutions A and B were passed, offering parishes the option of restricting the ministry of women in their churches, and the Act of Synod 1993 was also put in place creating the existence of 'flying bishops' for those who would not accept the episcopal ministry of bishops who ministered alongside ordained women. The first women were ordained as priests in Bristol, in March 1994.

In 2006, twelve years after the Bristol ordinations, General Synod agreed that admitting women to the episcopate was 'consonant with the faith of the church', and work then began on a further series of reports, meetings, working groups and debates. July 2010, though, marked a particular crisis. A draft measure made by the Revision Committee[10] was taken to General Synod in York for a vote. But a late amendment was added to the measure by the Archbishops, intended to offer further safeguards to those opposed to women in the episcopate, but with the unfortunate effect of suggesting a two-tier system of bishops: one level at which women could be admitted to the episcopate, and the other level a separate order of bishops set apart for men only, with the inbuilt option for people to traverse the authority of a female bishop should they wish.

Undoubtedly the amendment was put forward with benign intent, in an attempt to preserve the unity of the Church while also enabling women in the Episcopate. Yet the expectation, seemingly, was that people would not object to the idea of women being consecrated on a different footing as men, but accept it as a necessary compromise. What actually happened was that both men and women among the clergy recognised that the proposal would undermine not only any women consecrated under such legislation, but the validity of the orders of all women priests, and, indeed, all male priests and bishops who accepted ordained women. We had already experienced the difficulties caused by such compromises before: Resolutions A and B and the Act of Synod 1993 had been created to make space for those who felt the need for a male-only clergy, but their unfortunate side effect had been to undermine the authenticity of women's ministry as if, somehow, the girls were allowed to 'play' at doing something only boys could genuinely lay claim to. Now these new amendments brought the prospect of a two-tier system in which women would be consecrated but the recognition of their role and authority would be optional, creating a kind of complementarian theology by default.[11] Between 1992 and 2010, through years of negotiating and taking soundings from all over the Church, and the best efforts of people on all sides, those against women's ordination could not, or would not, compromise. But those in favour, remembering the struggles of the 1990s that were caused by a corresponding compromise, were unprepared to sign up to a system of second-class bishoprics for women.

It appeared in July 2010 that no one had anticipated the intensity of the negative response to the proposed amendments. The tone of the Synod was not merely one of disappointment at delay; the degree of outrage expressed by many clergy signalled that the process had reached a crisis point. There was a palpable loss of confidence and trust, and, in the months that followed, it became clear that events had triggered a depth of feeling, notably among women clergy, that they would no longer accept compromises that disenabled their ministry. But that was also the last meeting of Synod before it was dissolved for re-elections, so by the time the 2012 vote came a new Synod was in place. Objections to the ordination of women as priests and their consecration as bishops came from opposite ends of the theological spectrum, and for different reasons: for the more catholic-leaning objectors, the issues mainly revolve around historical continuity and sacramental representation; for the evangelicals who object, the issues have principally to do with gendered roles in leadership. Anecdotally at least, it is widely reported that Evangelical and Anglo-Catholic opponents had worked together, 'cutting a deal' as it were, to promote as many people as possible to the House of Laity in order to block the vote. Whatever the truth of that claim, it was indeed in the House of Laity that the vote foundered, with the result that the Church found herself not only immobilised internally, but with a profoundly limited ability to speak to the wider world.

This brief summary, then, is enough to demonstrate that neither the movement towards women in the priesthood and the episcopate, nor the theological arguments on which that movement is based, are recent anomalies. But while incremental steps have been made towards the complete acceptance of women's ministry since the beginning of their formal role in the Church of England in 1862, a point of stalemate was reached in 2010 from which the Church has seemingly not recovered.

I would suggest that waiting for a moment when the Church will move forward with one mind is, like the Mariner's ship, an idea removed from reality; the truth is that as long as we wait for complete unity on one issue, we will remain immobilised and parched on the silent sea. We need, rather, to allow ourselves to look for some signs of life, even if they initially seem threatening, to lead us out of paralysis.

Finding theological clarity

How do we break the deadlock, then? Sarah Coakley pointed out in a recent article that the debate has descended into theological incoherence[12]; John Milbank further commented on a tendency for bureaucracy to override theological concerns[13]. The failure to maintain a coherent theology is surely the most damaging aspect of the current situation, for without it the very essence of Church life is lost. This being so, it seems to me that any further debate is pointless until one vital issue is addressed. It may seem as unlikely a solution as the sea-snakes did to the Ancient Mariner, but it could, in its simplicity, be the point that gives clarity and focus to all other concerns: the issue is the 'process of reception'.

The process of reception is defined in the first report of the Eames Commission, and states that a decision may be made and acted upon by a Synod or Council of the Church without the full assent of all parts of the Church. Reception offers a way to move forward on an issue over which opinion is divided, allowing for a provisional decision to be made and acted on, subject to later review. A decision made in this way continues to be provisional until such time as the Church reaches a consensus of opinion as to whether to ratify or rescind that decision. The option to reverse the decision later is genuine.[14] But the success of the process depends upon all parties, even its detractors, treating the decision with true respect – in other words, not merely tolerating it while inwardly disagreeing, but entering into it and giving it the benefit of the doubt.[15]

The decision to ordain women to the priesthood was made on this provisional basis, with the understanding that, should the decision eventually be found to have been a step in the wrong direction, it could be reversed. In that case those women already ordained would retain their orders, but no other women would subsequently be ordained.[16]

Reception and the wisdom of Gamaliel

The idea of reception is illustrated in a much-loved story from the Acts of the Apostles.[17] Peter and a group of the apostles got into an argument with some of the religious authorities, whose levels of anger were rising, seemingly because they felt their integrity was being threatened. Things were on the verge of turning into a fight when Gamaliel, a leading Pharisee and a wise and respected member of the Council, stood to speak. After Peter and his friends left the room, Gamaliel addressed those who remained:

> 'Fellow-Israelites, consider carefully what you propose to do to these men. For some time ago Theudas rose up, claiming to be somebody, and a number of men, about four hundred, joined him; but he was killed, and all who followed him were dispersed and disappeared. After him Judas the Galilean rose up at the time of the census and got people to follow him; he also perished, and all who followed him were scattered. So in the present case, I tell you, keep away from these men and let them alone; because if this plan or this undertaking is of human origin, it will fail; but if it is of God, you will not be able to overthrow them – in that case you may even be found fighting against God!'

This advice, commonly referred to as 'the wisdom of Gamaliel', offers a principle whereby when new movements or new developments rise up, rather than stifling them in the name of integrity the best course is to allow them to develop, trusting God to ensure that what is good will grow, and what is vain and ephemeral will quickly wither.

The spirit of this kind of 'lived wisdom' is fundamental to the Anglican habit of appealing equally to tradition, scripture and reason – a practice usually attributed to Richard Hooker, although he himself never described it quite like that. Hooker affirmed scripture as containing all that is necessary to salvation; he was also clear as to the importance of tradition, and critiqued those on either side who placed such heavy emphasis on one or the other that their interpretation was distorted. His appeal to reason is implied within his method. The Anglican appeal to reason, though, is sometimes misunderstood as meaning theoretical reasoning. For Hooker and the early Anglican tradition, the appeal was to reason in the classical sense, not just of theory, but of participatory knowledge. To know something was not merely to be informed or to theorise, but to know from within, to participate in it – not unlike the *manière de vivre* (philosophy as a way of life) that Pierre Hadot argued for, or philosophical contemplation as practical, lived wisdom. It is reason in this sense that informs scripture and tradition in Anglican theology.

The idea of reception is very much in the same spirit, for the commitment to live into a new way of doing things opens up the idea that we do not know what is right solely by using our powers of intellectual reason to exegete scripture and tradition; our 'reason' is incomplete without finding in the experience of lived wisdom the confirmation of what, provisionally, we believe to be true.

The process of reception concerning the ordination of women, then, is very much in keeping with the appeal to reason in the true Anglican sense, in that serious reflection on the experience of having women in the priesthood is a necessary part of, and not a separate issue from, all our theorising over scripture, tradition and historical continuity.

The value of the process of reception was immediately clear in the first few years after the 1994 ordinations. There were some notable examples of leading Anglicans who, having initially been sceptical about ordaining women, changed their minds once they encountered women in the priesthood. The lived experience told them what their imagination could not: not only had the sky not fallen, but the priesthood looked more complete, more fully human to them, now it included women.

As the Rochester Report later reiterated, reception is an effective mode of discernment if all parties commit themselves to the course of action with an open mind to see whether or not the new move commends itself long term. Reception doesn't guarantee that the whole Church will end up in unanimous agreement. It does, though, mean that those who have deliberately excluded themselves from experiencing the ministry of women priests have not also excluded themselves from the experience of discernment in this agreed journey. Arriving at a decision after a lengthy period of reception, then, should involve weighing the range of opinion bearing in mind the extent to which people have genuinely countenanced, or consistently resisted the idea. It will inevitably mean that some who have genuinely taken part in the spirit of reception may still disagree; it would be unrealistic to expect complete agreement. But over the twenty years since 1992, the Church has moved dramatically towards being in favour of the ordination of women, so it would be reasonable to say that the mind of the Church has become clear, that reception is complete, and that 'it seems good to the Holy Spirit and to us'.

It seems to me that assessing this period of reception offers a clear way forward over the issue of women bishops. If we are agreed that, having tested the water since 1994, women are to be affirmed in their priest-hood, then there is no theological bar at all to them becoming bishops – for, as Sarah Coakley has so clearly expressed, 'there is no such thing, in a theo-logic of any veracity, of a legitimately-ordained priest who is inher-ently banned from the episcopate by gender.'[18] A similar point was made by Dr Muriel Porter to the Synod of the Anglican Church in Australia in July 2001, when they were considering the possibility of consecrating women as bishops: '… I have not presented the case for women bishops on theological grounds, because the theological debate about the ordination of women was concluded in this church once women were accepted as deacons and priests.'[19] The tortured question, then, of whether women may or may not become bishops does not really reside in yet another round of theological discussions, but simply in the affirmation or otherwise of the validity of their existing priestly Orders.

No time-limit was set for the process of reception. And perhaps it is the failure to give it a clear conclusion that has led us into a curious double-speak concerning women priests. In late November, in response to the failed measure at Synod, many bishops and dioceses made grand gestures of support towards their women clergy. Some threw lunches or champagne breakfasts, others sent cards or flowers, in the hopes of encouraging women not to be downhearted about the vote. Yet although the sincerity of these gestures is not in doubt, they highlight the fact that the church seems to project an unofficial view that the period of reception is over, while the official line remains that women's Orders are still a matter of debate. There is, then, an urgent need to reconcile the official and unofficial points of view.

Unity in diversity?

To suggest formally resolving and closing the period of reception raises the obvious question: what about the minority that disagrees? It does not seem good to them, nor to their sense of what the Holy Spirit says, to affirm the ordination of women. Can we, then, have two opinions living side by side in the same church?

It is one of the glories of Anglicanism that, since the unlikely achievement in Elizabethan England of founding a church that produced both political and religious unity, the Church of England has remained a broad church. Varying theological opinion is not merely allowed, but positively encouraged; there is room to disagree openly with one's colleagues and even one's bishop without fear of retribution. For priests in the Church of England, a vow of canonical obedience does not involve leaving your brain or your conscience at the door; priesthood, in our understanding, is a journey of reconciled relationship, not subservience. Should we, then, try to negotiate some settlement that will allow for two points of view to live side by side?

Undoubtedly, balancing a variety of theological inter-pretations can bring richness and depth. As John Mac-quarrie memorably pointed out, there are as many as 27 different variations on atonement theory – 27 distinct ways of expressing the impact on the individual, the church and the world, of the death of Christ.[20] In this case, multiple viewpoints are like seeing many facets of the same diamond; shades of interpretation that add up to a whole, but do not fundamentally cancel each other out. Theological variety can bring richness, then, but that is not at all the same thing as combining two theologies that are directly opposed to each other, which is what the Church seems to be attempting in the case of the minis-try of women.

It seems to me, then, that while trust and tolerance could and should make room for those who do not agree with the majority opinion of the Church, the last thing we should do is to legislate for dual opinion in such a way that the official belief of the Church contains an internal contradiction. We cannot have female priests and bish-ops, and not have them at the same time, because yes cannot also mean no. This does not mean that we have to create schism, but it does mean that in recognising a minority of dissent we must in no way limit the affirma-tion and authority of women who are ordained and consecrated. If those who dissent from the majority view are willing to stay under these circumstances, they should be welcomed with the greatest respect, tenderness and pastoral concern. They must not be overlooked, passed by in the street, left out of conversations and committees. It is not easy to be the overlooked minority; no one knows this better than women of my generation who have spent years of their lives carrying out a semi-realised vocation to ordination. Genuine friendship and trust is vital. The very fact that it is impossible to affirm two opposing ecclesiologies makes it essential to take care of the minority, and it is incumbent upon those who are of the majority view to include the minority.

Despite a certain amount of unpleasantness towards women displayed by a few, most of those who object to women in the priesthood do so not out of misogyny, but from genuine concerns of conscience. We owe it to those we disagree with to be tender-hearted, patient, and genuinely open to the idea that they may see things clearly that we do not; anything less than such an act of love and hospitality is a stunted Christianity. Nevertheless, we cannot move out of deadlock if we try to maintain the position that the Church authenticates two opposing theologies on an issue of Church order.

Unity, even if it is fragile, is worthy of our careful attention. It should be noted, however, given that the majority of the Church has agreed, that perhaps the minority might place themselves in a voluntary period of reception – saying, perhaps, 'we are not yet persuaded, but we will give this a chance'. If this were to happen I would be the first to rejoice.

Whose fault is it?

The arguments over this issue have often included a bitter edge. Women have been accused of being too ambitious, too feminist, not godly enough or out for equality at any cost, while rejoinders have sometimes included misplaced accusations of misogyny. Arguments made *ad hominem* or *ad feminam* only serve to keep us in deadlock. It is essential that we turn away from these and focus on the good of the Church. But the converse is not mere 'niceness'. It's the epitome of middle-class English politeness to be nice, to bite your tongue and not say the unacceptable. But the Anglican ideal of a peaceful, negotiated settlement is nothing so bland as that; if we allow Church to be deceived by a veneer of niceness covering over deep-seated disunity, we will remain in deadlock.

At some point in the last twenty years it seems that the Church allowed theological debate and spiritual discernment to give way to a kind of pragmatic approach that attempts to keep everyone happy. The fact is, though, that no one is happy, and a veneer of niceness is a thin substitute for the vigorous command of Christ that we should love one another. It is worth remembering that Christ gave this command precisely at the moment that his disciples were about to run off in different directions, betraying him as well as their trust in one another. 'Love one another,' said Jesus – not agree with one another, or compromise and be nice, but love one another, even if you are on the point of a temporary falling apart.

As idle as a painted ship upon a painted ocean

With all of this in mind, the only question that really pertains is how we find a route out of theological deadlock. Once again there is a parallel here with the Ancient Mariner. There is some ambiguity in the poem as to quite how the ship ended up lifeless on the strange ocean, where seemingly the only choice was death, or life-in-death. It is never made clear whether the disaster was the crew's own fault, or if not, whose fault it was. As the ship sailed towards disaster the sailors first blamed the albatross and cheered the Mariner for killing it; then they changed their minds, grieved the albatross and blamed the Mariner. The cause of their trouble then was never clear, and neither was the point at which the ship sailed across the invisible line. The question, in the end, was not what went wrong or whose fault it was, but simply how to get out of the impasse.

The Church's circuitous attempts to make yes mean no seem a little like 'life-in-death', and perhaps, like the Mariner, we will only be able to move forward if we cease attributing fault or guilt, set aside gambling with spectres of the past and instead look for where signs of life will lead us out of deadlock and towards a passage back to being Church.

Theologically, logically, then, we must decide: now that a generous period of time has elapsed, are we able to affirm that women's priestly orders are valid, or not? If we were to decide this whole venture was a huge mistake, we would have to make suitable provisions to enable those women who are ordained to work out their future, while not ordaining any more women. But if we decide to affirm them as priests, they may also be bishops. We need not spend further time discussing whether women should be bishops or not, or trying to create a new kind of bishop with limited powers. We just need to decide whether we were right to ordain women in the first place. Either we must affirm women as priests, including some as bishops, or not. Yes cannot equal no.

The terms of the process of reception continue to remind us that until reception is agreed to be complete we must all accept that any of us may be wrong. But over the past two years, all the dioceses of the Church of England were asked to debate and comment on whether they wished to see women consecrated as bishops, and 42 of the 44 dioceses replied in the affirmative. It seems fair to say, then, that the vast majority of the communicant members of the Church are in agreement that ordaining women seems 'good to the Holy Spirit and to us'.[21]

Chapter 2

A Dream Deferred

What happens to a dream deferred?

> *... Maybe it just sags*
> *like a heavy load.*

Or does it explode?
Langston Hughes

During the decades of debate about the place of women in the Church of England, the conversation has been punctuated, not just by periods of waiting, but by a sense that there is something inherently spiritual and virtuous about waiting. Whether silently or aloud, the impression is conveyed that in the face of one obstacle after another, the right thing to do is to keep waiting. 'Wait patiently', 'Wait on God', 'Wait and hope', 'Wait for the right time', 'Our waiting will not be in vain'.

Mostly these injunctions to wait are meant kindly and sincerely. From some, they are offered as an encouragement not to give up hope, not to leave, not to become despondent. 'Wait for God's time' seems to imply a belief that the time will come, if we will just wait for it. From others the same words are used as a way of putting off a decision in the hopes that if we wait a while longer then somehow we will be able to resolve the issue in a way that everyone is happy with. A difficult decision now could lead to some leaving the Church; since we don't yet agree, the logic seems to be, we must pray more, wait more, until we do.

Waiting on God

The discipline of patient waiting is vital to faith and to ministry. Sometimes we choose to wait because it is wise to do so, and sometimes waiting is forced on us – as C. S. Lewis once described it, you can turn to God in the moment of deepest need, and find 'a door slammed in your face, and a sound of bolting and double bolting on the inside. After that, silence.'[22]

Other matters cause periods of waiting: there used to be a tradition that people in public office would resign after making a glaring mistake, but at least there is still an enforced pause in such circumstances. The writer of Psalm 25 expresses this well, and suggests that the need to pause and reflect is a far more deep-seated and ancient instinct than we might suppose:

'... you are the God of my salvation; for you I wait all day long. Do not remember the sins of my youth or my transgressions; according to your steadfast love remember me, for your goodness' sake, O Lord!'

The Psalmist waits on God, praying for deliverance from external threats as well as inner demons: 'Do not let those who wait for you be put to shame; let them be ashamed who are wantonly treacherous ...'.

For Anglicans, waiting is not merely an optional spiritual habit, but is woven closely into our liturgical life. The seasons of Advent and Lent, Holy Week and moments within each of the Daily Offices, create the habit of waiting for us. Waiting on God is not passive, but active and attentive, preparing for whatever comes next with acute and careful listening. This demands energy, and the Psalmists knew this when they wrote about waiting on, or waiting for, God. They were not just idling the time away, but waiting for something particular to happen.

The rhetoric of waiting

Perhaps it is the importance of the discipline of waiting in the spiritual and liturgical practices of Christianity that makes it so easy, in the face of a difficult decision, to assume that the best thing to do is wait – and this has become almost a comic refrain in the Church of England's incapacity to resolve its acceptance of women's ministries. At every stage in the process, as each delay has been encountered, Church leaders haave urged us to 'wait for God's time'. It is as if the only proper or possible response, after decades of going round in circles, is to be patient; it seems to carry a hope that if we just wait long enough the problem will solve itself. This rhetoric of waiting is not unique to the Church of England. 'Wait', 'Be patient', 'Your time will come', 'When the time is right …'; these are all common responses when nobody knows how to fix injustice. The words may be meant kindly and sincerely, but too easily they become clichés employed to fill the verbal space when we don't know what to say, excuses to avoid facing the truth, platitudes to calm the anger and frustration of injustice, or tactics to stall progress and silence protest.

Although it is sometimes right to wait, there is no monopoly of virtue in patient waiting. To agree to wait beyond the point of acceptability requires a passivity that is profoundly bad for the soul. And in this situation the call to wait, and wait, and wait again carries an undercurrent of immense, disempowering betrayal.

A dream deferred

To wait through disappointments and broken deadlines while a resolution is repeatedly deferred is damaging to individuals, relationships and institutions. Extreme cases of a deferral of hope are seen when people spend large portions of their lives waiting for inquests or judicial reviews. Even when justice is eventually done, the tragedy is not lost on us as we watch people released from lengthy prison sentences following a discovery of a miscarriage of justice, or families who have waited many years for inquests to be revisited after murder or abduction cases. The already heavy burden of a tragedy or huge error is greatly compounded by those lost years; we feel the sickening thud of injustice as we realise that ten, twenty, thirty years of someone's life have been put on hold, and it comes home to us, as St Augustine put it, that 'the drops of time are precious to me'.[23] A recent example was the reopening of the investigation into the Hillsborough disaster. The panel, led by the Bishop of

Liverpool, uncovered the fact that what was already a great tragedy had been turned into a 'double injustice' through the failure of the original inquest to bring the matter to its proper conclusion. Countless other stories have appeared in the press in recent years of people who, having initially suffered terrible abuses, then lose years of their lives through a failure of process before they find the freedom that comes from proper attention being given to their situation, and a clear, just statement is made. What these cases have in common is that the original injustice, which is irreversible, is compounded by the deferral of justice and the years that are lost.

The delays over the ordination of women are quite a different situation; this isn't a physical, life-or-death matter, nor an event of sickening horror. The common thread, though, is the repeated deferral of a resolution. Here, too, endless delay gradually builds a sense of profound injustice that eventually has consequences, both on the individuals involved and on the spiritual life of the Church.

We should ask what we are doing to the Church as a whole, to dioceses and to parishes, as well as to individuals. We should ask whose lives are we putting on ice with this interminable discussion; and whose years of training and service, into which they were called by the Church, have since had their value diluted. I sat with a woman not long ago who has served for forty years, first as a deaconess, then as a deacon and a priest. She is one of life's true saints, her quiet and holy ministry invaluable to the many people who have walked through her doors. Yet in the midst of the endless rounds of discussions over female bishops, she said, 'I sometimes wish I'd left years ago. After all of this, they still don't think we are worth validating, and I wonder whether I should have left in protest instead of propping up a system that tells women we are second class.'

It is central to the Anglican understanding of a calling to ministry that a person's call is not received directly and individually from God; rather the call comes from both God *and* the Church. It is sometimes the case that a person does not recognise their own call until someone in the Church suggests it to them. And it is always the case that people's personal sense of vocation is tested to see where that call is best realised. Regardless of whether or not a woman hopes to be a bishop, then, her vocation cannot be fully realised unless it is fully recognised and endorsed by the Church.

Few women have any ambition to be a bishop (and in any case, as with men, it is usually those who are not ambitious for power who are better qualified for it). But the ongoing absence of women in the episcopate not only limits the ministries of a few women, it undermines the priestly vocation of all ordained women. If or when women become bishops, it will make almost no difference to what most clergy do from day to day. But for women throughout the Church, lay and ordained, it will make all the difference in the world to their sense of being received and valued by the Church. In the meantime, clergywomen live in a kind of 'limbo' that affects all of life now, because the Church that called them dilutes the validity of their orders by failing to resolve this issue.

God of the Rahtid

In the face of this 'limbo', then, calling on people to 'wait', as if this is a test of faith, is absolutely the wrong thing to do. We could draw excellent arguments for this from psychology, mental health, politics and anthropology – but more importantly for Anglicans, we can find reasons *not* to wait in tradition, reason and the Holy Scriptures.

'Hope deferred makes the heart sick,' says the writer of Proverbs, 'but a longing fulfilled is a tree of life.' Langston Hughes picked up this proverb in his famous poem, and teased out the psychology of political or structural oppression. 'What happens to a dream deferred?' he asks, 'Does it dry up, like a raisin in the sun? Or fester like a sore – And then run?' Waiting on God is one thing, but waiting interminably for a promise that, repeatedly broken, morphs into a destructive, pointless deferral, is not so much waiting, as wasting away. But if we refuse to submit ourselves to the destructiveness of just waiting patiently, what other response might we make?

Robert Beckford's imaginative and constructive theology is aimed at the experience of racist oppression, not gender-based discrimination. But some of his ideas make equally good sense in any situation in which a group of people has limits imposed upon it as a result of their inherited characteristics. In particular, Beckford contrasts two possible theological responses to oppression. He notes that one response has been for churches to focus on eschatological hope rather than on the expectation of change in the near future. Worship and preaching that place hope in the afterlife have the effect of pacifying what Beckford describes as 'low level rage', of removing the unholy spectre of rebellion or protest and replacing it with a prayerful waiting on God. When Christian tradition withdraws from political activism, and focuses instead on waiting for the Kingdom-come where there will be no more crying or pain, it can produce enough comfort to soothe and sublimate the rage. But although this keeps the peace, it neutralises any prophetic power for change. Beckford further explores the idea of 'redemptive vengeance' – a call, not to violence or anarchistic rebellion against God, but to respond *to* God with a sufficient level of protest and challenge to envision and create justice in the present. This will undoubtedly mean upsetting the status quo. But Beckford argues that anger can be harnessed as a source of redemptive power, a force that releases people from passive waiting and enables them to realise their proper place in the world.

In *God of the Rahtid*, Beckford suggests that rage should not be sublimated, but that it is precisely what could motivate the Church towards the prophetic task. 'Rahtid', a mildly offensive Jamaican/Caribbean expletive that expresses anger or outrage, is taken by Beckford to describe a radical and prophetic anger that steps outside the bounds of politeness, but can be seen in the work of Jesus himself, and is, arguably, the missing element in spirituality when the Church finds itself incapacitated to restore justice and freedom to the oppressed. In short, a polite and patient spirituality will create a church that waits for heaven, but only a spirituality that dares to get angry and overthrow some moneylenders' tables will be able to inaugurate the Kingdom of God on earth.[24]

This contrast between sublimated or harnessed anger also plays out in the imagery of *A Dream Deferred,* in Hughes' various possible outcomes of delayed promises. On the far extremes are a passive, depressed community that cannot flourish, and the destructive power of out-of-control rage. But in between is the intensification and building-up of the emotional power of redemptive anger that will constructively address injustice. And this is where Beckford's idea is located; in between the refusal of either passivity or anarchy, righteous anger can be focused to forge a pathway out of injustice and despair.

Churches may call on people to wait, and thus pacify communities and individuals into a mode of living that will merely survive oppression without completely losing hope, and without causing any trouble. But this kind of waiting does not ultimately bring about change; instead it prevents both communities and individuals from flourishing. Calling on the Church to wait, if that is simply a means of buying time and pacifying justifiable anger, is a mistaken and even destructive misuse of a spiritual discipline.

Nice girls don't get angry

Despite the fact that there is every reason – theological, ecclesiological, spiritual and psychological – to remove every bar to women in the Church's ministry, there is a further problem that underlies the question that is often levelled at women: why, now we are 'allowed' to be priests, do we have to ask for more? One female priest told me that, after she spoke up in a Synod meeting in favour of women in the episcopate, she was approached by a man in the coffee break who said to her, 'Why do you have to be so ambitious? We've let you women be priests – why can't you just be satisfied with that?'

This is not to do with scripture, or reason or tradition, but a pervasive cultural stereotype that makes it unacceptable for women to ask or demand, and even more unacceptable for them to get angry. The kind of persistence for justice that is considered strong and brave in men is often dismissed in women, who are perceived as being shrill, ambitious or demanding. And anger is even more complicated in this scenario, for not only does the Church have a complicated relationship with anger in general, 'girls' are supposed to 'play nice', and if they get angry they are often perceived as unspiritual.

Perhaps part of the problem is precisely that very churchy, and particularly English trait of 'niceness', which demands that we do not say or do anything that will offend or upset someone else. Yet think about this for a minute. 'Niceness' is not at all the same as courtesy and respect. Niceness leads us to give the benefit of the doubt when we should not, and it disenables us from challenging injustice. 'Niceness' and English politeness have been shown recently to have contributed to – even colluded with – some serious and tragic injustices. A worst-case example is the terrible abuses of children perpetrated by Jimmy Savile and other notable national figures, which were clearly seen and yet overlooked by people who didn't want to make a fuss. Clearly the situation of women priests is not usually on the same scale of abuse (although there have been stories of sexual harassment in vestries). The point, though, is not to compare injustices, but that 'niceness' and the reluctance to cause upset to others can be very destructive. We urgently need to get over niceness, and allow clarity of thought to surface and be expressed.

Redemptive rage, then, is highly complex, and difficult to bring to this particular issue. Women who are among the very best servants of the Church already find themselves constantly navigating disapproval that comes their way because they don't fit someone else's stereotypes. But they are further silenced by the Church's fear of anger, and the expectation that women should be soft, patient and undemanding.

Such caricatures reveal underlying sexist expectations (and, as Beckford points out, something similar happens with racial prejudice). But, with Beckford, I would challenge these expectations. Why is it considered not 'natural' or 'acceptable' for people to be angry over injustice? I am not in any way calling for riots or violence, or destructive acts. But clean, redemptive anger, and the action that it inspires, may be just what is needed to cut through the deadly combination of English niceness, and the sense of obligation – for women in particular – to remain passively accepting of the incoherent muddle the Church has settled into.

A silent exodus

Some women find enough support in their daily life to tolerate these injustices and continue with their work.

But some have left the Church, either through theological principle, or anger at the situation, or in some cases because they become depressed – unsurprisingly, since sublimated anger usually transforms into forms of grief, depression and despondency. Sadly, the Church appears not to notice. Between 1992 and 1994, elaborate and generous terms and conditions were offered to male priests who could not accept the ordination of women, to enable them to move to other churches without losing too much by way of income or pension. There is no corresponding offer made to women; but far worse than the lack of any practical measures is the apparent lack of awareness of a silent exodus of people who feel they can no longer represent a church that excludes or devalues women.

Much of this is, of course, anecdotal; there are no exact statistics to offer. But I know that even among the clergy I am not the only person who has left, gone abroad or otherwise moved sideways. I personally know seventeen priests – male and female – among my own circle of friends who have left parishes for other related areas of work such as chaplaincy, education or psychoanalysis, or have moved abroad in order to continue to serve as priests in places where these issues have already been resolved. I know eight more who say that if their family situation allowed it, they would do exactly the same. And I know of numbers of women who have quietly left the pews because they will not worship in a church that treats other women in this way. Under the surface, then, this is a more explosive and rotten situation than perhaps people acknowledge.

God waits for us

The rhetoric of waiting in this situation is a travesty of the spiritual discipline associated with such seasons as Lent, Advent or the Pentecost Novena. Instead, perhaps we should cast our eye over scriptural injunctions that indicate that God is, in fact, waiting for us. There are a number of places where waiting for something to happen reverses the dynamic: instead of the world waiting for God to intervene, act, protect, support or defend, as if initiative always comes from God, we see that God also waits for a human response.

Genesis 18 offers us a story in which God is presented in a curious juxtaposition as judge over the earth, the one who called Abraham and Sarah and will never break a promise, and yet also the friend of Abraham, to the extent that God is mutable – willing to mould the out-working of justice around the response of one person. A story such as this becomes a minefield if it is too directly and literally applied to modern life. Nevertheless, at the heart of the story is the idea that God is not in a hurry, and waits for human response, even to the extent that the outcome of events depends as much on human response as on divine will or guidance.

John 2 gives us the wedding at Cana, where Jesus famously turned water into wine; the first of his signs, according to John's account. Water into wine has so many layers of meaning; the idea of provision, of sacrament, and of the blood of Christ poured out. But there is also the curious moment of conversation where Jesus' mother presses him into action. Here, it seems, Jesus waited for the initiative of another person before he acted.

Hebrews 10 gives a theological account of the work of Christ in atonement, in which Christ's work is accomplished in principle, and yet its full realisation is still pending. In the midst of this gap between the future being settled and its becoming a reality, Christ, we are told, 'sat down at the right hand of God – and since that time he has waited for his enemies to be made his footstool …'. The argument of Hebrews proceeds with exhortations to the community to persevere in confidence. But it also intimates that perseverance – active waiting, if you like – is mirrored by the fact that Christ himself is waiting.

All these passages have multiple exegetical and hermeneutical possibilities, but they – and more besides them – are linked by the idea that not only do we wait for God; God waits for us – to have an opinion, to provide an answer, to take action, to do justice and love kindness. So the waiting and hoping and longing that we do meets with a corresponding waiting and longing in Christ, the implication being that we should pay close attention to see whether we should be waiting, or whether God is waiting for us.

The recognition that waiting is not unidirectional – not just us waiting for God – has a powerful psychological and spiritual effect. To wait interminably and then be repeatedly disappointed is not only to dull faith into passivity; worse, it pushes the responsibility for the deferral on to God, creating an image of a God who puts us 'on hold' with no certainty as to whether we are being attended to, or have simply been forgotten about. But the alternative – admitting that God is waiting for us – places responsibility on us to respond, and restores an image of God as justly, attentively and actively waiting to hear and affirm us. To pay attention to someone, and find that they are waiting for you, is a source of energy and hope.

Langston Hughes, in his short poem, summed up better than any philosopher or psychologist what happens to a dream deferred. His metaphors for delayed hope alternate between the imagery of decay (rotting meat, or a festering sore) and intensification (a raisin or a dissolved sweet becoming sweeter and more intense with passing time). But in each case, his point is that hopes and dreams do not remain static. A dream changes all the time. And his closing lines encapsulate the real challenge – does a deferred dream defeat the dreamer as it sags 'like a heavy load', or does it eventually build intensity to the point where it will bring about an explosion of energy?

As in Hughes' poem, the dream of women in ministry is not the same as it was twenty years ago, or a hundred years ago, not only because it has been held as a dream for a long time, but because the context in which it is now being envisioned has shifted another whole generation. When I was in high school, girls knew they would have to fight hard to get into university, since only one in four students at British universities was a woman, and even harder to find their place in professions such as law, research science, medicine or academia. Now, though, girls in high school see almost every path open to them. So the closed door of the Church is no longer one strand in a wider debate about the place of women in society; now the Church stands out as anachronistic, as the ground around us has shifted. The illogicality of the Church's thinking and practice is obliterating her effectiveness in the proclamation of the Gospel. The dream, by being delayed, has changed in nature.

When the Ancient Mariner saw the sea snakes and responded positively to that sign of life, suddenly he found he was able to pray again – which, within the poem, indicated a re-connection with the real world, and the recovery of speech, action, movement and life. For us, the time has come to stop covering over this turgid and depressing spectacle with a misguided call to wait for God's time and admit that God is waiting for us.

Chapter 3

A Personal Story

Tell me, what is it you plan to do
with your one wild and precious life?
Mary Oliver, 'The Summer Day'

So far I have ventured a little into theology, and into some ideas that frame our spiritual disciplines. Long-term decisions made by the Church cannot be founded on anything less than solid theological thought; decisions cannot be made to please individual people. But – returning to the idea of reason as lived experience – there is also a place for taking account of the way in which our theological and spiritual structures actually play out in real life. Experience is not enough on its own to guide the future direction of the Church, but it does provide a valid critique of theology and spiritual disciplines. For that reason, I think it worth relating some of my own experience of living with a calling before ordination was an option, then being one of the first women to begin theological college after the 1992 General Synod vote, and why I eventually felt that to fulfil my calling I had to work outside the Church of England.

Long before 1992 I was aware of a sense of calling. Since my teens I had been a natural leader with gifts in language, theology and the arts that fitted a preacher and a liturgist, and the nagging feeling that I should be doing something with it was like an itch that wouldn't go away. But the opportunities to explore those gifts within the Church were limited. As a teenager I discussed with two vicars, and then a bishop, what I might do with my sense of calling. The first vicar smiled benevolently and told me that vicars always needed good wives. The second vicar and the bishop took me more seriously, but both explained that while there were few restrictions on women who undertook missionary work, the best they could offer in a parish was practical contributions in my spare time, like organising rotas or teaching Sunday School. I tried some volunteer mission work, based first in London and then in Norway, but after a couple of years I realised that any long-term usefulness I would have was not going to be within any official structures. So I set about using my gifts elsewhere, and worked in the music business, singing, writing and working as a recording artist in a variety of different settings. During this time, I rented a flat in South London in Gilmore House, which, though I did not know it at the time, was the house in which Isabella Gilmore had trained her early deacon-esses. I toured and performed in all kinds of 'secular' venues, and increasingly I found myself working in religious broadcasting, or as a session musician for various well-known recording artists whose work was principally in contemporary worship. I played and wrote music for a variety of TV shows, and did a lot of work for BBC Religion for its radio programmes. In the midst of all this, my parish priest encouraged me to shoulder more responsibility in the musical life of the parish, which I did as time allowed.

In 1990 I went to visit my vicar. The liturgy my parish used was packed with great theology, and it combined various elements that reflected the multi-cultural setting of the parish. But somehow it was an unedited richness, and lacked the kind of organisational thread it needed to 'work' as a whole. With the eye of a writer and performing artist I was longing to get my editorial pen on to the script and refine it into something that had more coherence.

To my surprise, when I explained all of this, the vicar replied, 'So, you want to be ordained, then?' 'No, I don't,' I replied, 'and since I'm a woman that clearly isn't an option. But I really do want to make our parish liturgy way better than it is right now. We have so much of beauty, yet it's lumpy, and over-wordy, and illogical, and the beauty gets drowned out in the excess of text that needs editing. The music falls somewhere between classic and edgy, and we sound dated. I can do something about this, if only you will let me.'

'You *do* want to be ordained, then,' said the Vicar, decisively. 'You can't go messing about with liturgy unless you are ordained. The Church won't let you.' He pulled an ordinal off the bookshelf, and handed it to me. 'Go and read this,' he said, 'and then you will understand. And I will introduce you to some people in the diocese who can talk to you about vocation.'

I took the book home and read through the promises made at ordination, and began to understand what he meant. To lead the church in worship is central to what it means to be ordained. But although he was technically right, there was a problem – for this was 1990 and women could not be priests. I had made it thus far carving out a way to exercise ministry unofficially; I had no reason to assume anything would change.

Suddenly I found myself in a series of interviews with various diocesan representatives, and to each of them I told the same story. I knew God was calling me to be useful, and I wanted to have far more direct involvement in shaping the worship and mission of a parish. But I was wary of putting myself in a situation that was a kind of 'waiting room' for ordination, as I thought I might end up with less room to be useful to the Church, not more.

Every person I met in the Church – directors of ordinands, bishops, vocations officers, theological college teachers – said the same thing. 'We would like to consider you for the priesthood,' said one person after another, 'and we believe that it will not be long before women are ordained priests.' Gradually, I found myself in the curious situation of being called by the Church to a ministry that didn't yet officially exist.

As I travelled up and down the country to these interviews with people – mostly men, and just two women – whose job it was to decide whether I really was 'called' by the Church, I found they were almost unanimous. But the two people who did not agree with my call were my first brush with the kind of serious resistance that would later become a daily reality for me. The first was a man who took the view that it was not worth investing in me because (as he said) it wasn't cost effective to train women because they stop to have kids and then they retire early. 'But,' I protested, 'many women continue to work after they have children. And the law has changed on retirement – by the time I retire the age will be level. I have nearly forty years to give the Church.' He smiled, told me that I clearly didn't understand the law, and insisted that women retire at 60. How was it possible, I wondered, that men making decisions for the Church really didn't know that retirement law was changing, or that more mothers go out to work than stay at home? And how was it not worth investing in me, if I were to serve the Church for thirty-seven years? I couldn't help but think that Jesus, with his three-year ministry, would have failed to qualify. The second man I met was adamant that although I might make a nice pastoral assistant, he would not recommend me to take an academic course as he didn't think I was bright enough to keep up. Again, I was astonished. It was the 1990s and I had been offered a place at a Cambridge college. Yet a man would still readily assume that a woman wouldn't be able to cope with taking a degree?

My last interview took place on the morning of 11 November 1992, and after pausing to keep silence at a war memorial, I was driving back to London listening to the Synod vote on the radio. When it was announced that the vote had passed, and women would now certainly be ordained as priests in the near future, it had a more profound effect on me than I had anticipated. In national and international terms, I have always felt the historical weight of 11 November; not just as a declaration of freedom, but a line in the sand that no one ever meant to walk back over. I had stood at a memorial only that morning; and now on the same day I was overcome with a feeling that this too was a historic moment; that a decision had been made that would release the Church forever into a new freedom, a space in which faith could flourish like never before.

I optimistically believed that with that decision made, the recognition of women's orders would follow readily. But there is all the difference in the world between being allowed to enter a role, and being welcomed into it. It was played out in the press as if a long struggle had at last been resolved. In fact, for many of us, the struggle had only just begun.

∾∘∾

It was fascinating to arrive at theological college in 1993. The first women were to be ordained in the spring; some of them had already served for years as deaconesses and then as deacons, and there was something joyful about joining the long line of women who had blazed this trail.

Although one man on a committee had refused Church funding for my training, I was offered an alternative source of funding via my diocese, which, to my delight, came from the legacy of the same Isabella Gilmore whose house I had lived in previously, and who had spent her life training deaconesses.

About one in seven of the ordinands at college were women, and they included some of the finest women I have ever met: clever, kind, imaginative, determined and spiritually wide-awake. One Saturday in late September I walked around the beautiful city of Cambridge in the late summer sun; the next day, on Sunday afternoon, I attended the opening services and introductory events at the theological college, and all seemed right with the world.

Then Monday morning came. Arriving in advance of morning prayer, I opened the door to my study. There on the doormat was a leaflet. 'A woman's place is not at the altar but in the kitchen,' it read. 'Put on an apron, get back to where you belong.'

I didn't even know what to do with the leaflet under the door. Challenge it or ignore it? Make a fuss, or say nothing? It was my first day; it was both unnerving and unacceptable to have this happen, but already I was second-guessing how I would be received as a woman, and I didn't want to seem like a troublemaker or a campaigner. So I waited. A few days later it was my turn to meet with the Principal. He poured me a coffee and we had some genial conversation. He commented that it was a historic moment to be starting at theological college just as the first women were about to be ordained priests. How did it feel to be welcomed into the Church at this historic moment, he asked?

I pulled the leaflet out of my pocket and said that I was happy to be here, but there were some who were not so happy. I asked his advice on what to do with this distinct lack of welcome from fellow students. 'Ignore it,' he said. 'Once women are actually ordained that kind of treatment will quickly die out. All it will take is a few courageous women to keep their heads up and carry on.'

But it didn't die out. There were many good people there, and the lectures and the wonderful libraries were like a taste of heaven. But every day also brought me face to face with a determined campaign to undermine women. We were repeatedly left out, shouted down and overlooked, and *ad feminam* attacks were commonplace. A purely theological debate would raise comments such as: 'You would do better not to be such a bossy feminist', 'You should be concentrating on raising some kids' and 'It's not right that you take jobs from the men – you are emasculating the Church'.

Although I didn't realise it at the time, the leaflet under the door on my first day at college was a clue that this was going to be a tough vocation. For every person who, in the name of the Church, had called me into ministry, there was another determined to stop women from taking their place. Perhaps I should have known this. I'd been reading the Old Testament prophets for years, but I had read them with an optimistic lens, thinking that Bronze Age attitudes were behind us. Now, though, I think the prophets touch on an enduring truth about humanity: changing the law doesn't change the heart.

There were some moves in college to make liturgical language somewhat more inclusive; not to the extent of suggesting any female characteristics within the God-head, but in the effort to acknowledge that women were part of the human race. One morning I was walking downstairs towards the kitchen and heard the conversation going on inside. 'Just say "she" every now and then in the prayers,' one man said to another. 'That makes the girls happy. If they feel like we are including them they will shut up and we can do the real work without them.'

I don't much enjoy fighting, so I began to disengage from some of the theological college in-fighting, spent more time and energy in the Divinity Faculty and my Cambridge college, and just put my head down and worked. It wasn't entirely good for the soul, but was very good for my academic progress. Wherever there was a friendly face, I learned to give thanks and count my friends. But along with mastering theology, I also learned that among the clergy were some highly politicised people who were determined to reverse the decision made at Synod, and get rid of the women.

As time wore on I think some of those attitudes were chipped away a little. Some of the doubters began to realise we were going to serve, not overturn, the Church, and simply getting on with the job without engaging in a fight seemed at the time to be the best strategy. But the undercurrent of demoralisation continued, and almost without me realising it, I was being worn down in tiny, tiny increments.

Through internships, a first curacy and subsequent posts, I continued to encounter both a warm welcome from some, and quite punishing sexism from others. Whenever there were large processional events at Ely Cathedral, the Lady Chapel was assigned as space for clergy to robe. The very first time I took part, I walked into the chapel and found myself mostly among strangers, nearly all of whom were men. I put down my bags and introduced myself to the nearest fellow clergy member. He looked straight over my head to another man, as if I wasn't even there, and said, 'Did you hear something? I almost thought I heard someone speak.' Over the following few years, that stunningly beautiful chapel was repeatedly a place where I was ignored, talked over or through, as if I wasn't even there.

The communion rail is supposed to be the ultimate place of reconciliation, where people gather to embody their unity with God and with one another. I love presiding at the Eucharist, yet it has also brought stabs of pain. Countless times, I saw people stand or kneel at the rail, holding out their hands as if to receive. But the moment I held out the consecrated bread, they would refuse it, and pointedly turn their back and walk away. I was told many times not to take these protests personally: it was their way of making a general statement about women, not a personal slur. But I was the person actually standing there, and I am a woman. So even if their rejection was not directed specifically at me, it most certainly included me. When it happens week after week, it is not easy to shake off the feeling of rejection. More to the point, I am not sure it is possible to carry out genuine ministry and at the same time inure oneself to other people's feelings. Ministry is all about identifying with people, investing in them, walking beside them and carrying their burdens, and this is incompatible with maintaining complete emotional distance.

I believe most junior clergy make mistakes, even male ones. I know I am not the only person to have sung a note in the wrong place when singing the *Sursum Corda*[25] for the first time, or who needed to look at the script to say the absolution, or who has made some other ecclesiastical *faux pas*. But when I did make mistakes, correction would often not be simply an explanation of what I had done wrong. It would also include ridicule, and dismissive comments suggesting that this proved women are not cut out for the job; it would be followed by questions as to my vocation and my commitment to the ministry, and often criticism of my clothes for being 'too feminist', or 'too feminine' or 'not feminine enough' or 'too modern'. I was told on several occasions by senior male clergy that they would do everything in their power to make sure I never got another job. I was in vestries where I was ignored, harassed, ridiculed, sworn at, and, just once, spat on, by men who were neither more clever nor more called than I, but simply had louder voices, larger egos and an absolute determination that a woman was not going to join their club.

In the midst of all this, though, I also discovered outstanding and heartfelt support in other places. A retired bishop who lived nearby seemingly intuited that I was being given a hard time, and invited me round for tea regularly; he gave me endless encouragement, and taught me techniques for performing (in the right sense of the word) the liturgy with dignity and care even in the presence of people who wanted deliberately to derail me. One dean I worked for was not overly effusive in manner, but quietly and carefully, at just the right moment, gave me words of the most profound wisdom. Three of the tutors from my theological college (two of them outstanding women who knew these struggles first hand) kept in close touch and offered their wisdom and support. A number of members of the various congregations I worked in, and a whole host of fellow clergy, took the trouble to offer encouragement, humour, joy, prayers and all the other things you need in difficult circumstances.

I wavered sometimes between telling people how bad it was, and trying to change the subject. I worried that if I told the truth, or told it too often, I would lose the support or interest of those who were doing their best to walk alongside me; I found that telling the truth often reveals little 'clubs' of loyalty among male clergy and you need to be very sure who your friends are. I also felt that from my own point of view, if I talked about it too much it would submerge me completely, and negate all the good things I was discovering about the ministry.

The years I was in college, then, and the first few years after I was ordained were a massive struggle. Why didn't I just leave? I had good reasons. Firstly, I really did believe I was called, by God and by the Church, and ordination is not just a job contract – it is a set of vows. Secondly there were many, including the Bishops of Ely and Huntingdon and fellow clergy, who supported and encouraged me, taught me, prayed for me, and helped me to grow a thicker skin and rise above it. Thirdly, among the congregations I served were people whom I loved, and who loved me; how could I let them down just because a few people were bullying me on the side? My fourth reason was that, even among those who cannot accept women as priests or bishops, there are many who are kind and courteous, not misogynists or bullies at all. Given that it seems possible for people to disagree and yet still somehow support one another, I reassured myself that this was not a church at war, with clearly demarked sides. If some of those who doubted my orders were friends to me anyway, and found ways of working together respectfully, that seemed another reason to stay. But my final reason for staying was that I have always felt strongly that you shouldn't let bullies win; if you cave in to their bullying you make them stronger.

For all those reasons I stood my ground. I learned, even when I was fighting tears, to pull myself together enough to sing Evensong. I learned to preach the Gospel boldly and confidently while being stared down by people who were willing me to fail. I learned to stand up for other people even when I was pilloried for it by the few who were determined to push the women out.

I learned, too, how not to be frightened of people who threatened me with their power. Elizabeth Goudge once wrote: 'Truly great men and women are never terrifying ... Their humility puts you at your ease. If a very important person frightens you he is not great; he only thinks he is.'[26] Those who threaten or humiliate you to keep you in your place are not great; they are mean, perhaps insecure, certainly spiritually lacking. Unfortunately, though, such people sometimes have a lot of institutional power. So I had to learn how not to let them have power over me. I wrote out Goudge's words and pinned them above my desk, and determined not only to refuse to be intimidated, but also never, ever to wield what little power I had over other people; not to bully others as a kind of revenge on those who bullied me.

All of these were, I suppose, lessons worth learning. And I believe I did more than just survive. I think I grew stronger, and perhaps became a bolder and a better priest because I had to learn how to do it under stress. I learned how to stay solidly, calmly committed to the job under duress.

To find the strength to maintain one's self-confidence in the face of constant undermining may be a good thing in the long run, and to develop the absolute determination never to undermine someone else certainly is. But these were lessons learned at such deep personal cost that I sometimes wonder whether I should have left sooner. Little by little, I was worn down. The richness of life, the joy in the little things, got harder and harder to hold on to. I began to find I couldn't switch off when I was off duty. Living with the need to be permanently, unfailingly beyond rebuke is no way to live. From being a happy and relaxed person I had become wary, always watching my back, a little too wise, a little too perfectionist.

By the time 2010 rolled around I was in a better place, working in a kinder environment in a chaplaincy role in Cambridge, and beginning to recover some of the joy I had lost along the way. There were still times when I walked into church prejudice, but less often than in those earlier years. But the post was short-term, and in 2010 I had to start looking for a move. I ventured out with a few applications that would take me into a Church post. Perhaps, I thought, I had weathered the storms and the future would look better.

Meantime, discussions were moving forward concerning women in the episcopate, and while I have never felt much interested in being a bishop myself, I knew it would make an enormous difference to all female clergy (and to many Church members, male and female) to know that women at last were fully accepted as clergy. There are numbers of women my age and older who could walk into a bishopric tomorrow and transform the Church – because not only would they do a fantastic job, their presence would lift the cloud of unresolved doubt about the rest of us. Surely, women were not going to be held in doubt for another five, ten, fifteen years? Perhaps my theological college principal had been right, even if not about the timing – the reservations about women would dissolve in time. So I was cautiously hopeful as I sought my next post that the Church was moving in the right direction. And then the 2010 Synod came around.

The tipping point

When the 2010 Synod approached, and the Archbishops' amendment suddenly appeared, it seemed to me like a tipping point. As I noted in Chapter 1, I understood that the motivation behind the amendment was to hold the Church together. But it was also immediately clear to me that the result would be to exaggerate the two-tier system for women.

Why, I wondered, in bending over backwards to accommodate the detractors, did no one think it mattered to accommodate women? Why, in all the discussion of how terrible it would be if some male priests left the church, did no one seem to notice or care if women left? Seemingly it was assumed that we would, once again, 'play nice' – simply resign ourselves to the situation and carry on. Yet the women (and some men) who were already quietly leaving the Church through the back door were never even noticed.

Suddenly, instead of seeming that the Church was moving tentatively forward, it became apparent that we were going round in circles. The burden of it weighed heavy, both from a personal point of view, and for my position as a representative of the Church. Because the Church of England is a national, not a congregational church, many of the people a Church of England priest spends her time with are not regular churchgoers at all, but members of the general public. They are not well-read on the theological niceties of the discussion; instead all they see is a message the Church projects, albeit by accident not design: women are not that important. Almost every day someone asked how I could work in a Church that so blatantly devalued the work I was doing. Over and over again I heard myself explain that the legislation and practice was not truly representative of the Church's view of women. But gradually my words began to sound hollow, even to myself. There is a limited window of time during which an institution can justify a yawning gap between what it claims to believe and what it does in practice. Jesus was extraordinarily ahead of his time in his treatment of women, and so, despite popular caricatures of him, was St Paul. The Church of England had been making steps forward to bring these principles into line with present-day culture. But the compromises that promised a two-tier system for ministry effectively adopted a practice of complementarianism – in which women are deemed, in principle, to have particular roles assigned to them by gender. The undercurrent to all of this was that the legislation and practice of the Church produces an image of a God that is not the same as the God most of its members claim to believe in, and certainly not the God I believe in.

One of the recurring questions I ask of myself in the midst of ministry is how the work we do and the words we say speak of God. Theology does not only occur in our thinking about what we believe. The theological message that emerges in how we live perhaps speaks even more clearly of what we really believe than anything we might think or say. It seemed to me, in 2010, that the biggest problem of all in this unresolved debate was not how it limited individual clergywomen, or how it threatened to inconvenience those who prefer not to acknowledge women's ministry, but the picture it paints of God which is in direct contradiction to the theology we claim to believe in. If we really believe in a God who is powerful and just, creative and true, loving and wise, beautiful and mysterious, how dare we present to ourselves and the world such a pinched, narrow, mean picture of God?

The picture that emerged in the muddle of 2010 was not of a God of order, nor of a loving Father, but of a God who gives gifts to people only to take away the opportunity to use them; a God who places the divine image in both men and women, but then declares half of them substandard; a God who shares creation with all people, but then shuts the girls out and only allows the boys to play.

If women really had no intellectual abilities, no leadership gifts, pastoral instincts or theological acumen, then preventing them from taking part in ministry would surely be a good way of ordering the world. But evidently women do have all those gifts. Basing our ecclesiology on a pre-modern view of women makes no theological sense. This is not just a problem of logic (though it is that), it is a more critical problem about way we limit our portrayal of God, such that we project a theology that does not add up to the creative, generous, adventurous, loving, challenging, Holy and just God we claim to worship.

I began to question the amount of time and mental energy that I had been spending on surviving the unpromising circumstances. If there was any point in remaining in the Church, it was to serve the people, and offer my gifts and skills to those among whom I worked. If the Church was to continue to disenable women in the very ministry it had called us to, was there any point in staying? This conundrum is by no means new to women; it is older by far than the debate addressed in this short book. A thirteenth-century Flemish poet called Hadewijch struggled similarly with two opposite paths, neither of which were good ones. She neither felt able to force the issue and demand power, nor to accept the powerlessness the Church imposed upon her, for neither of these suited the demands of a godly faith. Instead she creatively forged an alternative theological path for herself, a determination to find an alternative way to live out a ministry. '. . . all that the forces of Love urge me to,' she wrote (and for Hadewijch, 'Love' means 'God'). 'They do not understand it, and I cannot explain it to them. I must then live out what I am; What Love counsels my spirit, In this is my being: for this reason I will do my best.'[27]

I considered whether I might find a third way of my own, as I had done in the early part of my career, or whether I should stay and put more effort into campaigning for the inclusion of women in the Church of England. I thought of those who had struggled with these issues long before me. What would Maude Royden have done? She campaigned on the one hand, but took a position as a preacher elsewhere because she knew that really her vocation was to preach more than it was to campaign. And I thought of Isabella Gilmore, whose legacy had supported me at theological college, just as she had supported her deaconesses in the 1890s. I was sure she would have frowned on giving up, but she was no stranger to finding innovative ways around the system to get the work done. I remembered living in her house during the years I worked in the music business, when I regularly created liturgies and worship materials despite the fact I was not ordained. I had not been ordained subsequently to become a campaigner, and if fighting for the right to work used up more energy than actually doing it, perhaps the time had come to take an alternate path, and work outside the system.

For me, then, watching the 2010 Synod was a defining moment. The Church's decision makers were trying so hard to please everyone that the Church was disenabling the vocation it had called women to. The dream had been deferred for too long, and it felt as though – quietly and in slow motion – something exploded inside me.

This is no easy decision for a priest, for priesthood begins with vows made by the priest to God and the Church, and by the Church to the priest. These vows are not indissoluble, but they are far more binding than a job contract. So no one whose Holy Orders have been taken in good faith will walk away on a whim. But, apprehensive as I felt about finding a new kind of work, I suddenly felt completely unafraid of the idea that I might somehow be abandoning my vows. For the first part of my life, I had to work out my calling elsewhere because the Church was simply not open to women. I knew perfectly well that it is possible to carry out one's calling in an apparently non-ministerial setting. Far from abandoning my call from God, I might fulfil it better by removing myself from the diminishing effect of the Church's ambivalence.

I went, of course, to talk to my bishop, for one of the vows one takes at ordination is the vow of canonical obedience. Having served under three Bishops of Ely, and three Bishops of Huntingdon, I have found every one of them to be supportive and kind, living up to their formal role as a 'Father in God'. This time was no exception. Bishop David listened to me for a whole hour, asked me searching questions, pointed out some flaws in my thinking and helped me to think clearly. And eventually he gave me his blessing to go and work out what to do next, with the assurance that he would pray and keep in close touch, and that my canonical residence[28] could remain within the Diocese of Ely until there was a good reason to change that.

So I began to look for work outside the Church. I sought writing, publishing, teaching or academic work.

By early 2011 I had come up with a combination of two part-time jobs, one academic and one in publishing, and a writing contract. It was going to be very tough, and I was going to be financially hard-up. But it seemed the best way forward.

I was on the verge of signing up to a package of non-ministerial work when the phone rang. Yale Divinity School was in need of a new Dean of Chapel and Professor of Theology – someone who could work in an ecumenical setting, with a combination of skills in liturgy, music and theology. I said no, thanks – I had just made my decision to walk away from formal ministry. But the dean of the school was persuasive, and talked me in to making a visit. God, it seems, has a sense of humour. Within six months I had a visa and a plane ticket to the United States.

I had imagined it would be interesting to work in another country, and particularly in an institution that is renowned for its radical inclusion of women. But I never anticipated what an absolutely transforming experience it would be to be treated automatically as an equal. It makes a huge difference on a personal level – heart, soul, mind and strength – to work in an environment where I am never treated with suspicion just because I am a woman. My competence is never questioned, my colleagues and my boss call on me constantly, and there is an easy flow of advice, collaboration and expertise among colleagues. Not once since I arrived here has anyone said 'you're not doing a bad job for a girl' (which, even said affectionately or in jest, wears a bit thin if you hear it every single week). Not once have I been overlooked in favour of a male colleague just because I am a woman. It is rare here for women to find themselves unable to make their voice heard. So, on a personal level, despite moments of deep homesickness for friends and family, and for English culture and countryside, I feel transformed by this move, and for this I am grateful.

But aside from the personal benefits to me, what I would love my colleagues in the Church of England to know is this: I achieve twice as much in a working week as I did before. Why? Simply for this reason: none of my mental energy is wasted justifying my existence, surviving bullies, fending off harassment or anticipating sexist behaviour. I don't have to think about whether I should speak more loudly or more softly to gain permission to be heard. I don't have to worry about whether my clothes will be thought too feminist or too feminine, or second-guess myself all the time to work out how to gain the space and the permission to do the job I'm appointed to. I just wake up every day feeling good, go to work full of energy, work hard all day, and come home, most days of the week, still smiling. It's not that I have an easy job – in fact, some of my colleagues tell me it's one of the toughest jobs in the school. I preside over all manner of community disquiet, liturgical disagreement, theological debate, student heartache and pastoral distress; the deadlines are tough and the work is never-ending. Some days I do a great job, and some days I just do OK. But there is a complete absence of the barrage of doubt, discouragement and personal attack based on something I cannot control: the gender I was born with.

I currently live in a kind of ecclesiastical limbo – I still belong to the Diocese of Ely in England, and have not relocated to a new church. How my future relationship to church will work out remains to be seen, and this is one of the matters that occupies me on my current walks along the beaches of Long Island Sound.

But I also sometimes try to imagine how different my first twenty years in the Church might have been, had the positive atmosphere I currently enjoy been more present in my places of work then. I wonder how much creative energy is being poured away even now within the ranks of the Church of England, and how many women working devotedly in parish or diocese are having the quality of their work diminished by the demoralising atmosphere? How much energy, skill, spirit, morale and goodwill would be unleashed if the Church of England simply stood up to this negative treatment of its women, and said 'no more'?

I wonder how many more have, like me, felt the need to walk away because our service was received with such ambivalence – the warmth, so often expressed on a personal level, being undone by the institution's inability to make the acceptance official. More than anything, I wonder why it is that still, twenty years after the 1992 vote, the Church cannot bring itself to act decisively over whether it really wants women in its ranks or not. The House of Bishops is in favour, the House of Clergy is in favour, and so are 42 out of 44 dioceses. Yet seemingly no one has the power to make it happen. Of course I understand that the ways of the institution are labyrinthine. Nevertheless, I do believe that if there is a will to make it happen, it could happen swiftly. I hope those who make decisions on behalf of the Church of England will have the courage to make this a reality for one-third of her current clergy workforce, and for more than half of her total membership.

ﻌﻮﻋ

I watched the most recent chapters of this story, running up to the 2012 Synod, from the far side of the ocean. The proposal this time was another muddled compromise, and it was hard to know whether to hope it would fail, because it would reinforce a two-tier system for women, or hope it would pass, because of a sense of urgency to get something done. In the event most people seemed motivated by the sense of urgency, and committed themselves to voting in favour of the measure. But despite the majority of Synod voting in favour, the measure failed in the House of Laity. The shock-waves were felt far beyond the Church; the national and even international press were full of the story for days afterwards, and the discussion was picked up in Parliament.

This round of the debate saw many of the old chestnuts replayed; women were accused yet again of being ambitious, feminist, demanding, ungodly. This kind of talk seems particularly out of place in an institution which is supposed to embody, above all things, the way God values people. The damage is compounded by the fact that the Church doesn't seem to register how demeaning the situation is for women, and meantime it appears that the Church remains incapable of making a clear decision, while still people speak from pulpits about waiting on God, about vague assurances that it will get better in time, and encouraging women not to be too down-hearted.

What a different church it would be if all the gifts of its women were validated, and all their energy unleashed. If no more time was wasted discussing whether or not our place in church is valid; if no more goodwill dribbled away because of the despondency that follows from a dream being deferred, what a powerhouse of transforming social and spiritual power the Church might become.

If this is to happen, though, it will demand more than a compromised measure through the system that gives an impression of permission to women. And, in fact, it will even demand more than a simple, clear measure that authenticates women's ministry. It will actually require proper attention to the fact that the whole system is riddled with sexism. Even some of those men who are happy to vote for the full inclusion of women will have to change their habits, and recognise that it will take a generation of deliberately changing the culture before we can really say we have an inclusive church. Only when women can speak boldly without being thought of as 'shrill', only when they can dress in a variety of styles without assumptions being made about the quality of their work, when they are automatically included in committee meetings, or are as likely to be called for advice as their male peers – in short, when they can expect their working conditions not to be limited because of their gender, only then will we be able to say we have a healthy church. To achieve this will require something even more difficult than passing a piece of legislation.

But, because I am now living in an institution that has achieved this, I know it can happen. The Revd Grace Sentamu-Baverstock once memorably said in a church meeting that the Church of England is like a world-class ocean liner powered by the engine of a lawnmower. I would give anything to see that equation reversed. And the Church already has enough power to do that: it resides in all the 'wild and precious lives' of her members.

Conclusion

I come into the presence of still water.
Wendell Berry, 'The Peace of Wild Things'

1862 was a notable year. Claude Debussy and Gustav Klimt were born, Louis Pasteur and Claude Bernard completed their first pasteurisation test, and Alexander Parkes publicly demonstrated the first man-made plastic at the Great International Exhibition in London. Across the ocean the American Civil War was under way, fighting to end slavery, and in Ohio, Mary Jane Patterson became the first black woman to graduate from an American college.

1862 was the year Elizabeth Ferard was licensed as the first deaconess in the Church of England, and also the year Frederick William Faber published his well-loved hymn, *There's a wideness in God's mercy, like the wideness of the sea*. This confluence of events poignantly highlights the conflict of interest the Church struggles with. For, a hundred and fifty years later, we are still prevaricating over what to do with women. But the conflict is between women who wish to realise their calling, and others who feel that should that happen, they will feel conscience-bound to leave. Faber himself was an Anglican priest, but by 1862 when Ferard was licensed, he had seceded to Rome along with others from the Oxford Movement. The ebb and flow of church angst hasn't changed much, it seems. But in 1862 Debussy had not yet written his music, nor Klimt painted his masterpieces; plastic had not yet changed everything from medicine to space travel, and no one could imagine that women – who didn't yet even have the vote – might not only graduate from college, but become first-class academics. A lot of things have changed in a hundred and fifty years, but the fact that people come and go from different churches because of doctrinal disagreements hasn't changed at all.

We sing Faber's hymn often in my new chapel, and it puts me in mind of all those times I stood on the beaches in England in the early 1990s, soul-searching, watching the waves, and listening, as R. S. Thomas put it, 'to the swell born somewhere in the Atlantic rising and fall-ing'[29]. Little did I imagine that twenty years later I would be watching a synod debate from the other side of the Atlantic. But I do not regret my self-imposed exile. Twenty years may not be a long time in the span of history, but it is a big slice of one person's life. And while I believe in sacrificial faith, I think there is a place for asking ourselves whether the sacrifices we make are really what God is asking of us, or whether we are wasting our true gifts by making martyrs of ourselves. Looking back across the ocean, although I know I would be welcomed home should I want to return, I know that, paradoxically, it is only outside the walls of the Church of England that I am free to realise the call the Church placed upon me. The situation brings me pain as well as joy, and I am reminded of George Eliot's Dorothea, who, having moved to the other side of grief was not 'over it' but was able to live with it:

> '[Dorothea] felt as if her soul had been liberated from its terrible conflict; she was no longer wrestling with her grief, but could sit down with it as a lasting companion and make it a sharer in her thoughts.'[30]

But although moving across the ocean has provided a solution for me, it doesn't begin to solve the problem for my Church, which I still love and belong to despite an exile of sorts, and which I long to see freed from the impasse it is currently in.

So where does the Church of England go from here?

The way out of the impasse is going to cause some pain. Some people are not going to get what they want, but perhaps it's time to admit that is unavoidable whether we change or stand still. Above all, it is a matter of urgency to make a simple and clear decision. Anything less than an uncompromised acceptance of women in the episcopate will leave us motionless for another decade or two, while the energy and effectiveness of the Church's ministry leeches away. The only other option is to reverse the decision of 1992 and cancel any future ordination of women. There is no middle choice that will free us from the deadlock; we can only move forward if we admit that we cannot believe in opposing things at the same time.

The challenge before us, then, is not how to create an ecclesiastical system that admits opposing theologies, but to ask all people either to compromise their own wishes sufficiently to live with something slightly other than their ideal world, or to receive help and kindness as they seek another church home. As Faber himself wrote, after seceding to Rome, 'There's a *kindness* in God's justice, which is more than liberty.'

So, if the Church were to go with the majority view, what would happen to those who do disagree? For a few, the demands of their consciences may lead them to the harder choice, and they will feel that they must find a new church home. If they do, I hope and trust that they will be treated with the same kindness with which my own bishops treated me: with time to talk, a listening ear while they decide on their direction, and a blessing should they decide to leave.

Even with uncompromised authority given to women, I do not believe that all who disagree would have to leave. But the only way to go forward together is to ask all parties to proceed with trust and respect for difference. I am well aware that among those who still feel they cannot accept women in Holy Orders (indeed, some are friends and I care about them specifically), there are many who are nervous that trust is not enough. But endless talk of more laws, regulations and legally-binding promises sounds far more like a divorce than a marriage.

Of course, it is important to enable detractors to find a way of living within the Church despite not personally welcoming the authority of those women who become bishops. But for some, it should be enough to provide the tacit and binding agreement that parishes may, if they wish, choose to call only male priests to serve them. It is not necessary to create a church within a church to do this. There are many parishes in the Episcopal Church where this happens already; they are not the ones that hit the headlines, but they simply and quietly get on with what they do, and the Church at large understands and respects their choice to remain conservative on this issue within a church that has formally endorsed the ministry of women.

'We make God's love too narrow,' wrote Faber in his hymn, 'By false limits of our own.' I hope that the next generation of priests, bishops, deacons and laity in England will live to see a return to the spirit of generous hospitality that was envisaged in the establishment of Anglicanism, instead of the narrow limits that have reduced both our fellowship and our effective ministry. I don't want anybody to leave, but neither do I want to see the Church held together by a desperate network of compromises that, beneath an impression of unity, is really a negotiated settlement for warring factions to live together in the same house.

Whatever decision we make (including the decision that is made by trying not to make a decision) there will be some who feel they have to leave. There are already those who, like me, have been pushed to leave by the repeated deferral of a decision. If the Church decides to consecrate women, there may well be others who will feel they too must leave. But I have found in my own experience that making a choice, however painful, leads to the discovery that – in Faber's words – God's mercy really *is* wider than the sea. There is more goodness, life and hope in making a decision and moving on it than in remaining in deadlock. 'There is room for fresh creations,' wrote Faber. Accepting that a decision will involve some pain would still be better that trying to make 'yes' equal 'no', and thus remaining stranded forever on a lifeless ocean.

At the end of a service I presided over during my last month in England, a seven-year-old girl was leaving with her parents. In clergy tradition, I always greet people as they come in and out of church, and I make a point of talking to children as well as adults. As I said goodbye to this little girl, she put out a hand and touched my white cassock alb. 'Are you a bishop?' she asked. 'No,' I said, kneeling down to talk to her at eye-level, 'I'm a priest.' She looked at me, wide-eyed, as I told her just a little, in seven-year-old language, about what priests do. 'I liked watching you today,' she said. 'Can I do that when I grow up?'

With all my heart, I hope she can.

Maggi Dawn
December 2012

Notes

1. Tyndale, An *Answer unto Sir Thomas More's Dialogue*, Walker, H. (ed.), (Cambridge: Cambridge University Press, 1850),176ff.

2. Marius, R., *Thomas More* (New York: Collins, 1984), p.425.

3. The beginning of Church of England convents only slightly predated this, the earliest being founded in the 1840s.

4. (1825–1883)

5. (1842–1923)

6. MacCarthy, F., *William Morris: A Life for our Time* (London: Faber and Faber, 1994) p. 531.

7. (1876–1956)

8. Chisholm, Hugh (ed.), *Encyclopaedia Britannica* (11th edition) (Cambridge: Cambridge University Press, 1911).

9. The Representation of the People Act (1928) gave the vote to all women over the age of 21. Ten years earlier in 1918 a limited number of women were given the vote, provided they satisfied certain conditions of age, property ownership and marital status.

10. GS 1708–09Y: Draft Bishops and Priests (Consecration and Ordination of women) Measure; Draft Amending Canon no. 30; Illustrative Draft Code of Practice.

11. Complementarianism regards specific gender roles as God-given; its claim is that while all are equal in value in God's sight, men and women have different roles. Men are always thought of as the leader, 'head' or final authority in any social structure. Where complementarianism is adopted within church communities, it is generally only applied to family and church structures; thus it is common to find churches that have no problem with a woman being a solicitor or a GP, but will not allow them to hold a position of authority in the family or church.

12. Sarah Coakley, 'Has the Church of England finally lost its reason? Women bishops and the collapse of Anglican theology', ABC Religion and Ethics, 23 Nov 2012 http://www.abc.net.au/religion/

13. John Milbank, 'Unrepresentative laity: The women bishops debacle demonstrates why bishops need more authority', ABC Religion and Ethics, 23 Nov 2012 http://www.abc.net.au/religion/

14. See *Women in the Anglican Episcopate,* Anglican Book Centre, 1998, p. 26.

15. The idea of reception, and its various interpretations, is discussed at length in Chapter 3 of *Women Bishops in the Church of England? A report of the House of Bishops' Working Party on Women in the Episcopate* (Church House Publishing, 2004).

16. The introduction of so-called 'flying bishops' was also subject to a process of reception. These are bishops who are available to function as episcopal authority for those who are so completely opposed to the ordination of women that they cannot accept the authority of a male bishop who has ordained women. See Ven Judith Rose, 'Discussion paper on *Women Bishops in the Church of England "Rochester Report"* ', Fulcrum, 2005. http://www.fulcrum-anglican.org.uk/

17. Acts of the Apostles, 5:17–42.

18. http://www.abc.net.au/religion/articles/2012/11/23/3639111.htm

19. Dr Muriel Porter, in a speech given to the Synod of the Australian Anglican Church, July 2001.

20. John Macquarrie, *Principles of Christian Theology* (2nd edn.) (New York: Charles Scribner's Sons, 1977).

21. Acts 15:28 is a New Testament example of the idea that God guides through both human reason and the leading of the Holy Spirit.

22. Lewis, C.S., *A Grief Observed* (New York: Harper & Row, 1961), p.18.

23. Augustine, *Confessions* 11:2

24. See Beckford, R., *God of the Rahtid* (London, Darton, Longman and Todd, 2001), pp.38–65

25. The opening lines of the prayer sung or said at Holy Communion.

26. Elizabeth Goudge, *The Joy of the Snow* (New York: Coward, McCann & Geoghegan, 1974) p.212.

27. Harvey, A. (ed.), *Teachings of the Christian Mystics* (Boston & London: Shambhala Publications, 1998) p.84.

28. Canonical Residence refers to the fact that every practising Anglican priest has to be connected to and authorised by a Diocese.

29. Thomas, R.S., 'The Other', *Collected Poems 1945 – 1990* (London, J.M. Dent, 1993).

30. George Eliot, *Middlemarch*, Book 8, chapter 80.

DARTON · LONGMAN + TODD

Darton, Longman and Todd is as an internationally-respected publisher of brave, ground-breaking and independent books on matters of heart, mind and soul that meet the needs and interests of ordinary people.

Our books are written by, and for, people of all faiths and none. We believe that spirituality and faith are important to all people, of all backgrounds, and that the wisdom of any one culture or tradition can inform and nourish another.

We also publish the Jerusalem Bible, and its revised and updated successor, the New Jerusalem Bible – one of the most clear, accurate and distinguished modern English translations of the Bible.

For more information on DLT, and to buy our books, please visit our website
www.dltbooks.com
or visit your local bookshop. You can stay up to date with our activities by following us on Twitter @dlt_books

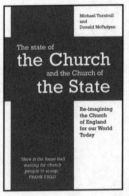

DARTON·LONGMAN+TODD

JOHN SENTAMU'S FAITH STORIES
20 True Stories of Faith Changing Lives Today
Presented by the Archbishop of York, John Sentamu

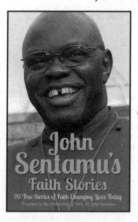

The most authentic stories of Christian faith in the 21st Century come from the experiences of 'ordinary' people living 'ordinary' lives.

In this unique book compiled by John Sentamu, the Archbishop of York, 20 people with everyday lives, families and jobs explain what their faith means to them and how it makes an extra-ordinary difference.

Some of these people face up to difficult personal circumstances on a daily basis – such as the widowed mother of two young boys, or the former soldier whose fellow soldiers were killed – others work for social justice in their local communities or use their unique gifts to communicate the good news of the gospel. All these stories are inspiring demonstrations of Christian faith in everyday action.

Includes a photo of each subject and personal introductions written by John Sentamu.

978-0-232-52978-4
£8.99
Order from www.dltbooks.com or contact
Norwich Books and Music at
orders@norwichbooksandmusic.com or on 01603 785925

DARTON·LONGMAN + TODD

Other DLT titles include: